Adult Coloring Book Stress Relieving Floral Designs Volume 1 Flowers in the Garden

Nisita Noojui

Adult Coloring Book Stress Relieving Floral Designs Volume 1: Flowers in the Garden

Copyright: Published in the United States by Nisita Noojui
Published November 2016

ISBN-13: 978-1539959953

ISBN-10: 1539959953

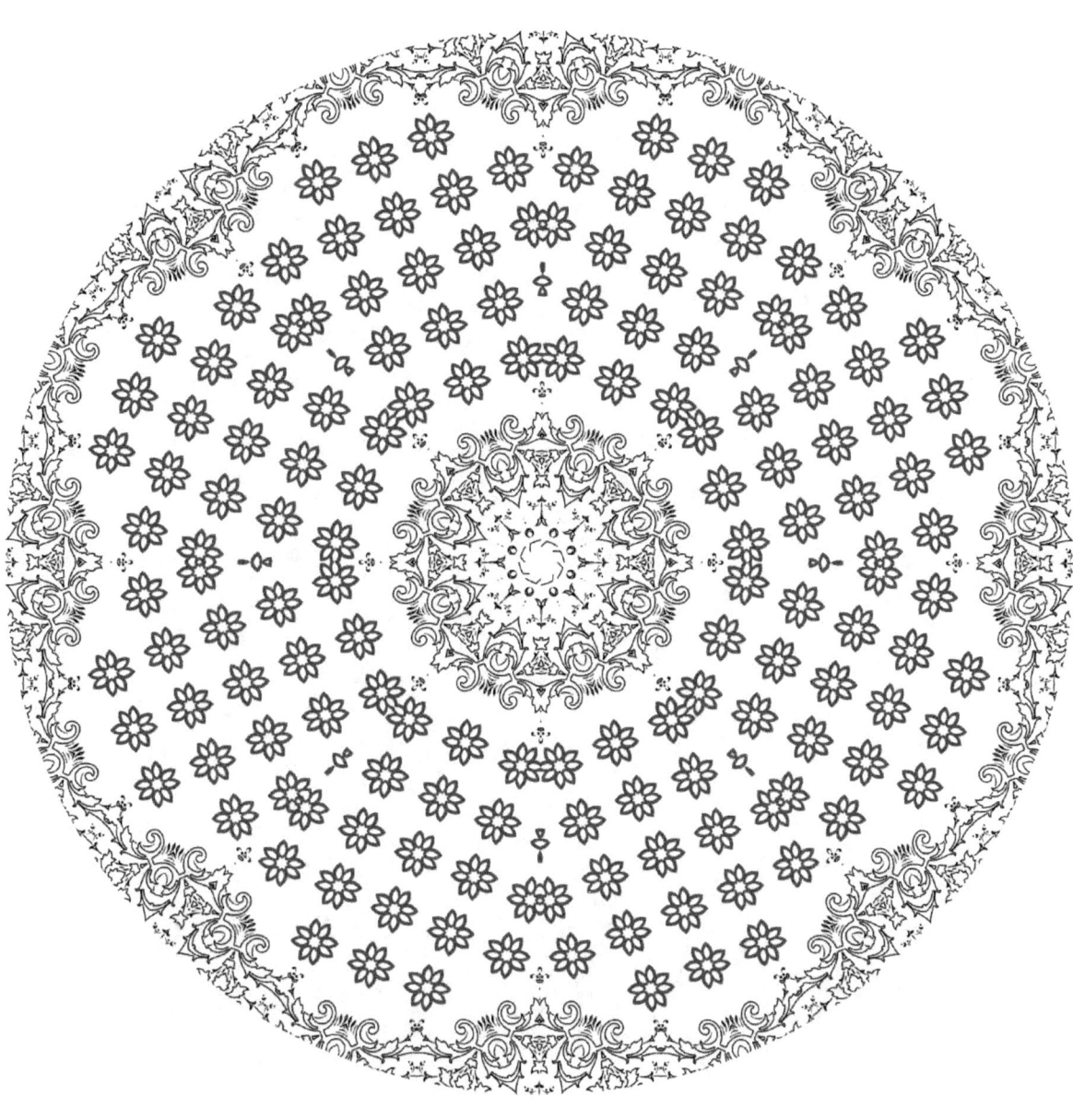

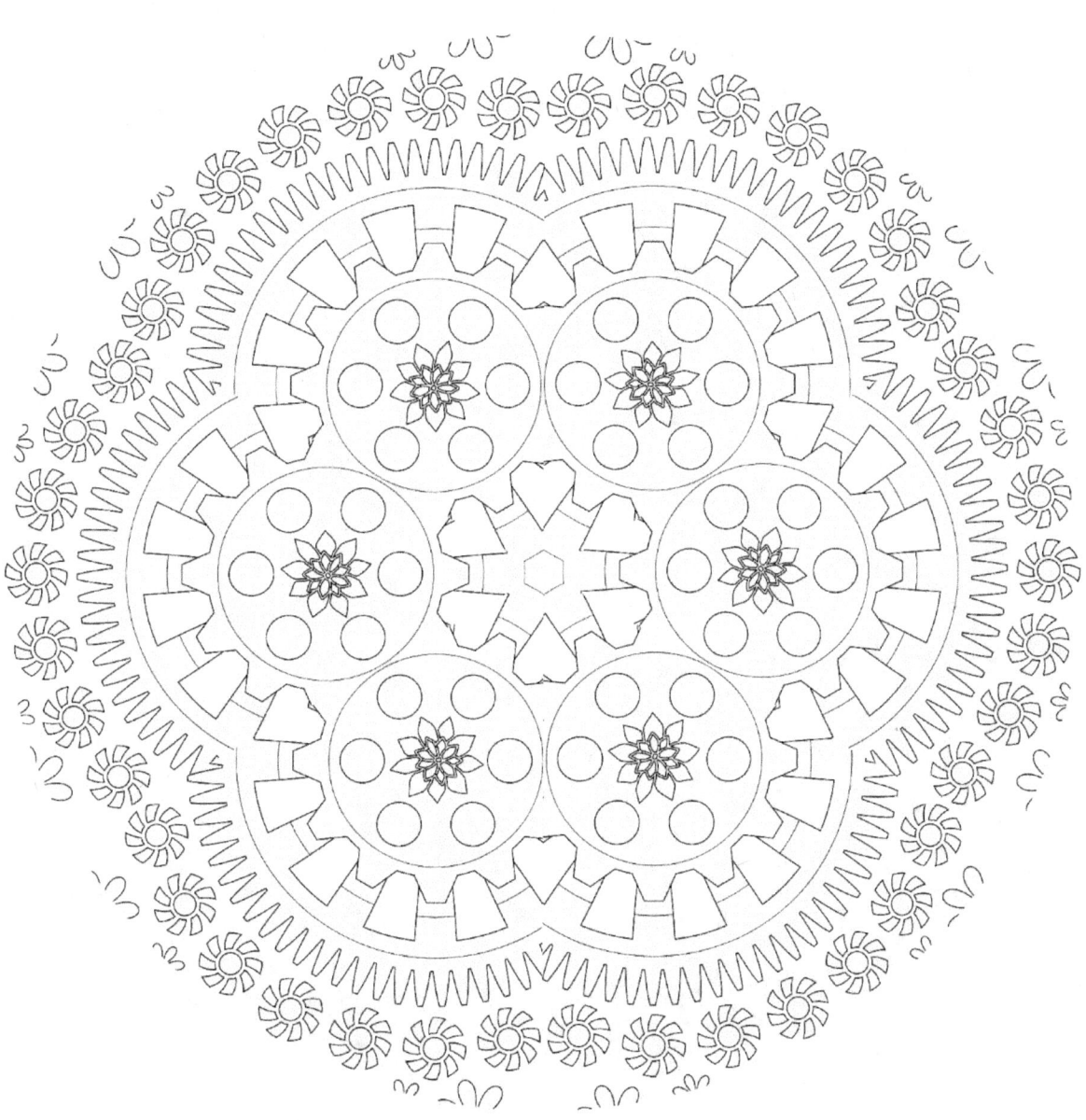

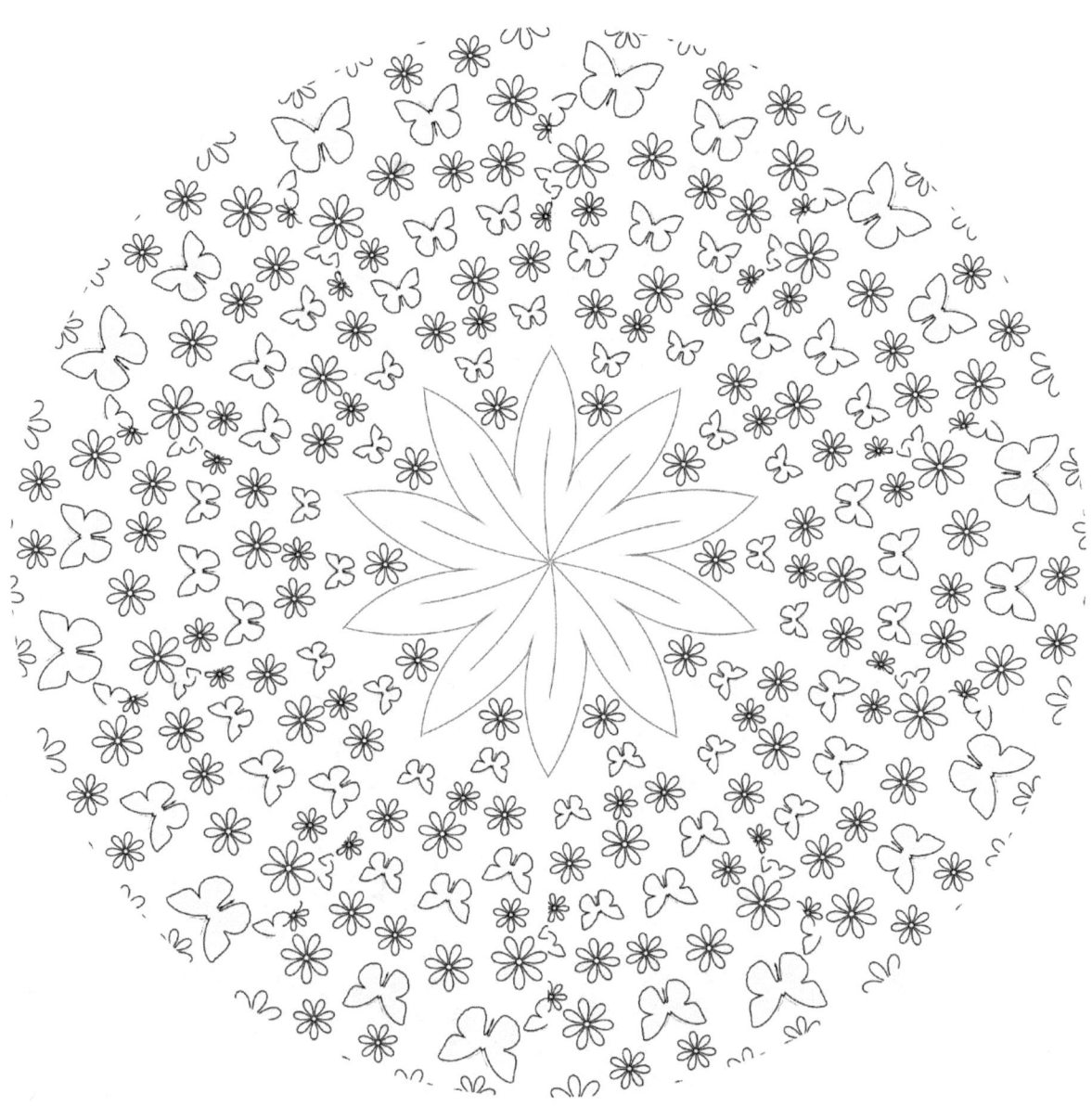

Thank you